I0096595

ADRIANA LUNA CARLOS
Editor-In-Chief, Designer
and Co-Founder

HANNA OLIVAS
Managing Editor
& Co-Founder

NICOLE CURTIS
Director of the SRS
Magazine Division

VITALITY
DIGEST

**ADVERTISING
OPPORTUNITIES**
Info@SheRisesStudios.com

CONTACT US
SheRisesStudios@gmail.com
www.SheRisesStudios.com

VITALITY DIGEST MAGAZINE
JANUARY 2025

SHE RISES
STUDIOS

www.SheRisesStudios.com

LETTER FROM THE EDITORS

Dear Readers,

Welcome to the January 2025 edition of Vitality Digest Magazine! As we step into the new year, we're excited to help you embrace a New Year, New Vitality. This issue is all about renewal, growth, and setting the stage for a vibrant year ahead. Packed with expert advice and inspiring stories, it's the perfect companion to kickstart your journey to health, success, and transformation.

We're thrilled to feature Carmen Maendel, an extraordinary fitness coach and CEO of Nate's Property Maintenance LLC, on our cover. Her inspiring journey of balancing business leadership with a passion for fitness embodies the essence of vitality. Carmen's story will empower you to take charge of your health and success, proving that vitality is the key to thriving in both your personal and professional life.

As we look ahead to 2025, we explore the latest fitness trends and the profound connection between health and productivity in business. This issue will help you integrate wellness into every part of your life, ensuring that you can achieve your goals with energy and focus. Plus, don't miss the details inside about our EmpowerHer Content Day in Las Vegas on February 22, 2025—an event designed to propel your success and well-being.

Thank you for joining us in welcoming this New Year, New Vitality. We're here to help you thrive and make 2025 your best year yet. Let's embark on this exciting journey together, nourishing our bodies, minds, and souls with every step we take.

Warm regards,

Adriana Luna Carlos and Hanna Olivas
Editors of Vitality Digest Magazine

FENIX TV

SHE RISES
STUDIOS

EMPOWER**HER** CONTENT DAY

at WELCOME TO Fabulous LAS VEGAS NEVADA

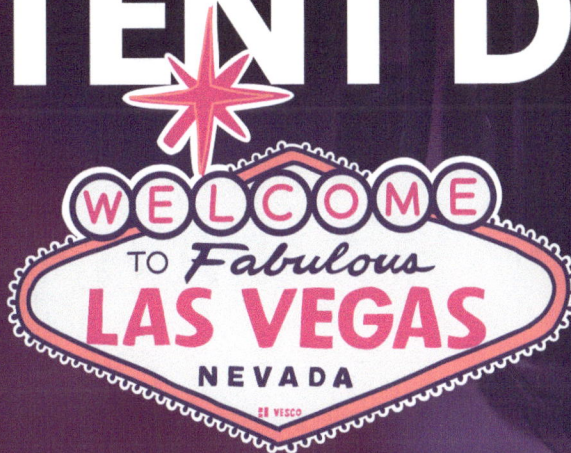

Elevate Your Brand Through Creative And Impactful Content!

EmpowerHer Content Day equips attendees with the tools and knowledge needed to craft compelling content for social media, podcasts, and videos.

FEBRUARY 22, 2025

TOTAL ACCESS TICKET: $127

WWW.SHERISESSTUDIOS.COM

Photo Credit: Erin Heemstra

HEALTH, FAITH, AND PERSEVERANCE IN BUSINESS

by Carmen Maendel

Carmen Maendel's journey as a fitness coach and her unwavering commitment to health and wellness have shaped her role as a leader at Nate's Property Maintenance LLC. Together with her husband, Nate, Carmen integrates the same energy and discipline that defined her eight years at Maendel Fitness into their growing business. For Carmen, health is more than a personal priority; it's a foundation for success in both life and business.

Carmen's passion for fitness has equipped her with the perseverance and dedication necessary to navigate the challenges of running a company. She and Nate approach every obstacle with the same determination they apply to their fitness routines, grounded in their faith and guided by their belief in treating others with kindness and respect. These principles have fostered strong relationships with clients and team members, reflecting Carmen's philosophy of service beyond mere transactions.

Each day for Carmen begins with intentionality. Before taking on the demands of running a business, she starts with her morning routine, which she credits for her mental clarity and physical stamina. Carmen begins her day with prayer, visualizing putting on the "full armor of God." Following a light breakfast and a greens cocktail, she heads to her home gym for a focused workout, alternating between high-intensity interval training, strength exercises, and core work. This morning ritual not only strengthens her body but also provides an opportunity to pray for her loved ones and reflect on the day ahead.

The discipline Carmen cultivated as a fitness coach still guides her approach to client relationships. At Maendel Fitness, she supported over fifty women in achieving their health goals through strategies such as SMART goal setting and personalized coaching. These same principles are evident in her business today. Carmen applies her understanding of balance and boundaries, emphasizing hard work while recognizing the importance of rest and recovery. She and Nate work diligently during the week and ensure their weekends include moments to recharge, whether through boating, horseback riding, or simply enjoying quiet time.

Carmen's focus on balance extends to her partnership with Nate. As co-leaders of Nate's Property Maintenance LLC, the couple prioritizes clear communication, mutual encouragement, and a shared commitment to health. While Nate's physically demanding role requires stamina and strength, Carmen's administrative responsibilities demand focus, energy, and a structured approach. Both understand the importance of a good night's sleep, balanced nutrition, and faith in maintaining peak performance.

Beyond her personal health practices, Carmen strives to create a well-rounded, positive environment for the entire team. She shares fitness and nutrition tips with workers and ensures they have access to high-energy snacks to stay fueled during long days. Safety and preparation are integral to Nate's fieldwork, and Carmen matches that level of care by maintaining a clean, organized workspace at home.

From scheduling clients to handling compliance paperwork, she has established systems that keep the company running smoothly.

Carmen's understanding of the connection between physical well-being and productivity influences every aspect of her leadership. She believes that health is not just a personal responsibility but a key factor in team success. When everyone—from herself and Nate to their team members—is physically and mentally well, the company thrives. Her leadership philosophy focuses on uplifting and supporting the team, treating them with the same respect and care she extends to clients.

For Carmen, the lessons learned in her fitness career remain deeply relevant. She sees challenges not as setbacks but as opportunities for growth, whether in personal health or business. Her advice to other entrepreneurs is rooted in this perspective. She encourages maintaining a balance between work and rest, viewing challenges as a chance to improve, and leaning on faith to navigate difficult times. Carmen believes in the importance of turning off "work mode" to relax and recharge, a habit that has helped her and Nate maintain a strong work-life balance.

Photo Credit: Heidi Adele Photography

Looking to the future, Carmen is committed to expanding Nate's Property Maintenance LLC while keeping health and wellness at the forefront. She envisions purchasing new equipment to ease the physical demands on their team and adding new members to better distribute the workload. Health, both physical and spiritual, will remain a cornerstone of the company's mission. As Carmen puts it, the *"muscle of prayer"* is the strongest one she and Nate will continue to build.

Carmen's story is one of dedication, faith, and balance. Her ability to integrate her passion for fitness and wellness into her business leadership has not only shaped her own journey but also inspired her team and clients. At Nate's Property Maintenance LLC, Carmen ensures that service truly means more than a transaction—it's about building strong relationships, fostering growth, and honoring the values that define her life.

Photo Credit: Erin Heemstra

CONNECT WITH CARMEN

www.natespropertymaintenance.com
www.facebook.com/profile.php?id=100093303554586
www.facebook.com/ncmaendel
www.instagram.com/maendelcarmen

REDISCOVERING STRENGTH: HOW RESILIENCE SHAPES YOUR PATH TO SUCCESS AND VITALITY

by Tammy Gibson

Life's toughest trials have the power to reveal our hidden strengths. My journey—marked by hospitalization, limb loss, and a series of life-altering health complications due to atypical COVID-19—taught me this in profound ways. After contracting COVID, I faced multiple severe health challenges, including the amputation of my right leg and nerve damage in my hands. The virus also led to a Stage 4 kidney injury, leaving me dependent on dialysis and uncertain about the future of my health. Through these intense experiences, I learned that resilience is not just a mindset; it's the fuel that keeps us moving forward with passion and purpose, even when obstacles feel insurmountable.

The journey of healing my body from COVID's complications, especially my kidney injury, was a lesson in patience, self-care, and faith. This period in my life taught me that the body and mind are capable of immense healing, but they need active support and care. I committed myself to restoring my health—not just surviving, but genuinely living. By embracing lifestyle changes, leaning on my faith, and holding a strong belief in my ability to heal, I began to see improvement. I learned that vitality is something we actively pursue and protect, even in the face of overwhelming odds.

Vitality is deeply tied to resilience, and both are essential for success in life and business. As a resilience advocate and business mentor, I guide professional women to tap into this inner strength and redefine their purpose. My programs, Captivate and Reimagine, are designed to empower high-achieving women to embrace self-discovery, build a personal brand that resonates with authenticity, and shine confidently in their careers. In our sessions, I help them explore how life's challenges can be transformed into resilience, empowering them to thrive personally and professionally.

A key component of my own resilience journey has been my commitment to physical fitness. As soon as I was healthy enough, I prioritized regular workouts to rebuild my strength. For me, the gym is more than just a place to exercise; it's a sanctuary where I reconnect with my body, focus my mind, and reclaim my power. Every workout reminds me that I am capable, progressing, and that healing is a journey rather than a destination.

Physical training has strengthened me not only in body but also in spirit, teaching me valuable lessons about perseverance, consistency, and discipline.

These lessons from the gym directly translate into my work with clients. In business, just as in fitness, success is built through small, consistent efforts over time. There are no shortcuts. We have to show up regularly, even on days when motivation is low or self-doubt creeps in. It's about pushing through discomfort to reach new levels of growth. This philosophy shapes how I mentor professional women: I encourage them to recognize their resilience, stay committed to their goals, and embrace the process, even when progress feels slow.

I work with ambitious women who seek a life of purpose and vitality. They are business owners, corporate leaders, and professionals who want to make an impact, but they need the right tools to push past limiting beliefs and embrace the full depth of their resilience. Together, we transform these beliefs into strengths, allowing them to lead with confidence, authenticity, and vision.

In helping women reclaim their vitality, I've found that the journey starts with owning our struggles. Every setback is an opportunity to grow, redefine ourselves, and create a legacy of strength and purpose. Vitality is not just about health; it's about living a life that truly resonates with who you are. It's about feeling strong, capable, and aligned with a purpose that drives you forward.

As I continue my own journey, I'm grateful to share these insights with other professional women. When we combine resilience with purpose, we unlock a powerful force that not only fuels our growth but inspires those around us. Vitality is more than a state of being; it's a choice, an act of courage, and a commitment to living life to the fullest.

CONNECT WITH TAMMY

www.toughliketammy.com
www.youtube.com/@toughliketammy
www.linkedin.com/in/toughliketammy
www.instagram.com/toughliketamm

LONG COVID NEARLY KILLED ME, NOW I'M TAKING BACK MY LIFE, AND YOU CAN TOO

by Lynette Milakovich

On April 7, 2021, I woke up with brain fog, neuropathy, tinnitus and insomnia without any explanation. This is all too common of a problem in America, as more then 20 million adultsare suffering from long COVID. I had lasting symptoms including loss of cognition, attention and retention. As my symptoms persisted, tremors developed, and I even collapsed a few times. Like 66% of people with long COVID, things took quite a dark turn for me with bouts of depression, anxiety, suicidal ideations, PTSD and apathy. My family was really worried about my health.

I spent more than a year and a half of my life in constant pain and agony. Under the advice of my primary care provider (PCP) and a psychiatrist, I tried treatment plans including COVID treatment centers, endocrinology, ENT, acupuncture, naturopath and IV therapy. Not only was there an emotional toll these false hopes were causing for me and my family, but even with insurance I spent almost $20,000 out of pocket for these failed treatment plans.

Life's biggest passions fading away.

Before the day that my symptoms began, I had a cross-country move planned for Florida that I was looking forward to. When I made the move, the symptoms persisted and eventually long COVID forced me to give up my career. I was a court reporter for more than 40 years, something I was unable to do with my symptoms. I was no longer able to be involved in relocating and packing my home for the cross-country move, and teaching yoga was a lost cause. However, the hardest part was the loss of connection with the people I love. I could not play an active role in their lives. I was a shell of the person I once was.

Finding the right treatment plan for me.

After the move to Florida, I began looking for a naturopath and was recommended to a pulminary specialist who gave me my first long COVID diagnosis. My first sign of hope came from a conversation with my neighbor, who was going through the medical program at Aviv Clinics in The Villages, Florida and suggested I give it a try. After doing thorough research, I went through the initial tests with the doctors at treatment center. The doctors analyzed my SPECT scans and blood, and it was confirmed that I was suffering from long COVID. Hyperbaric oxygen therapy (HBOT) was not a treatment I had previously considered but based on the success stories I had seen of other clients with long COVID I decided to give it a one last ditch effort. After the initial tests, I began the intensive 12-week medical program.

Getting life's simplest joys back.

I can now finally say that my life is back on track. While I do still deal with tinnitus, the rest of my symptoms are gone. I decorated my house. I've started cooking again and now have the energy to play with my first grandson. I'm teaching yoga again and have even returned to high-intensity workouts. My husband and I both know that Aviv Clinics saved my life, and I'm just so thankful every day.

Validating those with long COVID.

I have become passionate about helping those around me who are struggling with the effects of long COVID. It is important that providers worldwide acknowledge long COVID and diagnose it instead of making patients think it's all in their head. Patients deserve to be validated because this is a real disease that needs to be treated. I learned the hard way that early diagnosis is key. There are resources out there for everyone, including the Frontline COVID19 Critical Care Alliance. I did my research, and I was able to heal. When I remember the obstacles, I had to go through to be where I am today, thriving in retirement in my new state of Florida and picking up new hobbies, this is somewhere I never dreamed I would be at the beginning of this journey. There is hope for the millions of people suffering from long COVID.

CONNECT WITH LYNETTE

@LynetteMilakovich

MINDSET MATTERS:
HOW EMBRACING POSITIVE THINKING CAN HELP YOU AGE BEAUTIFULLY

by Beverly Little

Aging is inevitable, but how we experience it is largely shaped by our mindset. While society often emphasizes the physical aspects of aging, from wrinkles to gray hair, research shows that our mental outlook can profoundly affect how we age—mentally and physically. Studies indicate that individuals who embrace a positive mindset tend to experience improved cognitive function, better physical health, and enhanced emotional resilience. These benefits not only allow us to age more gracefully but also enrich our overall quality of life.

The Science Behind a Positive Mindset

Our thoughts are powerful. Emerging research highlights how a positive mindset improves cognitive function as we age. A study published in the Journal of Personality and Social Psychology found that individuals with a more optimistic outlook tend to have sharper cognitive abilities in later life. Positive thinking is associated with lower stress levels, which play a crucial role in maintaining brain health. When stress is minimized, the brain is better able to focus, remember, and process information.

Furthermore, a positive mindset can lead to better physical health. Optimistic people often engage in healthier behaviors, such as regular exercise, balanced nutrition, and preventive healthcare measures, all of which contribute to longevity. According to research by the American Psychological Association, those who maintain a positive outlook on aging tend to live longer, healthier lives. They experience fewer cardiovascular problems and lower risks of chronic illnesses like diabetes or hypertension. This suggests that how we think about aging can directly impact our body's ability to stay strong and resilient.

Resilience: The Key to Aging Gracefully

One of the most significant benefits of a positive mindset is its impact on emotional resilience, defined as the ability to effectively adapt in the face of adversity, trauma, or significant stress. As we age, we encounter various challenges—loss of loved ones, health concerns, or changes in our career and social roles. These experiences can take an emotional toll, but resilience helps us navigate them with grace.

Resilience is not about avoiding hardship but rather learning to respond to it in a healthy, constructive way. Individuals with a positive mindset are more likely to view challenges as opportunities for growth rather than obstacles. This shift in perspective allows for better emotional recovery and the ability to find meaning even in difficult times. As a result, resilient people often maintain a stronger sense of purpose and well-being as they age, allowing them to face life's challenges with confidence.

Cultivating a Positive Mindset for Healthy Aging

Adopting a positive mindset is not about ignoring life's challenges or being unrealistically optimistic. Instead, it's about choosing to focus on possibilities, growth, and the good in any situation. Here are a few ways to cultivate this mindset:

- **Practice Gratitude:** Regularly reflecting on what you're grateful for can shift your perspective and reduce negative thinking.
- **Stay Active:** Physical movement, whether through exercise or engaging in hobbies, promotes both mental and physical well-being.
- **Connect with Others:** Social engagement fosters a sense of belonging and support, which is crucial for emotional health.
- **Embrace Lifelong Learning:** Keeping the mind active through new experiences and knowledge keeps cognitive functions sharp and enriches your sense of purpose.

Aging beautifully is about more than just skin-deep changes—it's about maintaining mental clarity, physical vitality, and emotional resilience. By embracing a positive mindset, we can not only enhance our quality of life as we age but also navigate the complexities of growing older with grace, strength, and optimism. How we think truly shapes our age, proving that mindset matters more than we may realize.

CONNECT WITH BEVERLY

www.mindsetsoulshifting.blog
www.facebook.com/mindset.soul.shifting.coaching

SHE RISES
STUDIOS

FENIX TV

WE WISH YOU A

Happy New Year

Wishing you a year filled with
new **hopes**, new **dreams**,
and new **achievements**.

www.SheRisesStudios.com   www.fenixtv.app

FUELING YOUR BODY RIGHT: NUTRITION TIPS FOR A YEAR OF VITALITY

by Bharathi Ramesh

Stepping into 2025, many of us are prioritizing health, energy, and well-being. The cornerstone of achieving these goals is nutrition. The food we consume fuels our bodies and minds, playing a vital role in how we feel and perform every day. Let's dive into expert-backed nutrition strategies to make this your healthiest year yet.

1. Start with a Balanced Plate

The foundation of a nourishing diet lies in balance. Use the MyPlate method as a guide:

- **Half your plate**: Colorful vegetables and fruits. These are rich in vitamins, minerals, and antioxidants that support immune function and combat inflammation.
- **A quarter of your plate**: Whole grains like quinoa, brown rice, or whole wheat bread. They provide sustained energy and essential fiber.
- **A quarter of your plate**: High-quality protein sources, such as lean meats, fish, tofu, beans, or lentils. Protein is essential for muscle maintenance and repair.[1]

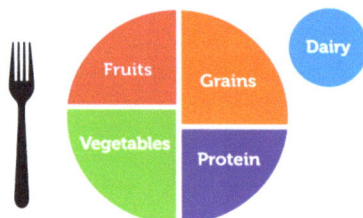

2. Prioritize Protein-Rich Meals

As we age, maintaining muscle mass becomes critical. Ensure you're incorporating protein into every meal: For example:

- **Breakfast**: Greek yogurt with chia seeds and berries.
- **Lunch**: A quinoa and chickpea salad.
- **Dinner**: Grilled salmon with steamed broccoli and sweet potato.

Including a variety of protein sources ensures you get all the essential amino acids your body needs.

3. Embrace Healthy Fats

- Fats often get a bad reputation, but healthy fats are crucial for brain health, hormone regulation, and energy.
- Incorporate avocados, olive oil, nuts, seeds, and fatty fish such as salmon or mackerel.
- Omega-3 fatty acids found in fish or flaxseeds can improve heart health and reduce inflammation.

4. Stay Hydrated

Even mild dehydration can impact your energy levels, focus, and metabolism. Aim for:

- 8-10 glasses of water daily.
- Add natural flavors to your water, like cucumber slices or mint, to make it more enjoyable.
- Include hydrating foods such as watermelon, cucumbers, and oranges.

5. Include Functional Foods

Functional foods provide additional health benefits beyond basic nutrition:

- **Turmeric**: Contains curcumin, an anti-inflammatory compound.
- **Fermented foods**: Yogurt, kefir, kimchi, and sauerkraut improve gut health by supporting a diverse microbiome.
- **Dark leafy greens**: Spinach and kale are rich in iron and folate, supporting energy and cellular function.

6. Reduce Processed Foods

- Highly processed foods often contain added sugars, unhealthy fats, and artificial additives.
- Swap chips for air-popped popcorn.
- Replace sugary cereals with oatmeal topped with fresh fruit.
- By reducing processed foods, you'll lower your risk of chronic diseases and feel more energetic.

7. Snack Smart

Healthy snacks maintain energy levels and prevent overeating at meals. Great options include:

- Handful of almonds and a piece of fruit.
- Veggie sticks with hummus.
- Hard-boiled eggs or string cheese.

8. Plan Your Meals

Meal planning can save time, reduce stress, and ensure you stick to your nutrition goals:

- Dedicate a day to prepare meals for the week.
- Store pre-portioned meals in containers for easy grab-and-go options.
- Try batch-cooking soups, stews, or grain bowls.

9. Listen to Your Body

Your body's needs can vary daily. Practice intuitive eating:

- Eat when you're hungry and stop when you're full.
- Recognize emotional eating triggers and find alternative coping strategies, such as walking or journaling.

10. Make Nutrition Fun

- Enjoy the journey of nourishing your body.
- Experiment with new recipes and ingredients.
- Take a cooking class or try a new cuisine.
- Share meals with loved ones to build positive associations with healthy eating.

Good nutrition is a cornerstone of vitality, confidence, and well-being. By focusing on balance, hydration, and whole foods, you can step into 2025 feeling your best. Remember, small, consistent changes lead to sustainable results. Let's fuel our bodies right and make 2025 a year of vitality!

CONNECT WITH BHARATHI

www.linkedin.com/in/bharathiramesh96
www.holisticlivingwithbharathi.com

FUELING YOUR BODY RIGHT: NUTRITION TIPS FOR A YEAR OF VITALITY

by Elizabeth Katzman

Over the years, I've seen a dramatic transformations in women who shift their mindset from deprivation to nourishment. This is especially crucial during perimenopause, when our bodies need more support than ever. The key? Prioritizing protein, managing blood sugar, and maintaining strong bones and muscles through proper nutrition and exercise.

The Power of Protein

Adequate protein intake is non-negotiable during perimenopause. I recommend 1 gram of protein per pound of body weight daily. This isn't just about maintaining muscle mass – protein plays a crucial role in hormone production, neurotransmitter balance, and blood sugar regulation. When women increase their protein intake, they often report feeling more satiated, experiencing fewer cravings, and maintaining stable energy levels throughout the day.

Beyond Calories: Understanding Blood Sugar Balance

During perimenopause, our bodies become less efficient at regulating blood sugar. This isn't just about diabetes risk – it affects everything from mood swings to hot flashes. By combining adequate protein with healthy fats, we create meals that provide sustained energy and support hormone production. This approach helps reduce anxiety, a common perimenopausal symptom, by providing the building blocks for neurotransmitters that promote calm and stability.

The Fiber Connection

Fiber isn't just for digestive health – it's crucial for hormone balance during perimenopause. As progesterone naturally declines, we can become estrogen dominant without proper estrogen metabolism. This is where fiber becomes our ally. It helps remove excess estrogen through the digestive tract and supports our estrobolome – the collection of bacteria in our gut that metabolize estrogen. Aim for diverse sources of fiber through vegetables, fruits, and legumes, to promote optimal gut bacteria diversity.

Strength Training: Your Metabolic Ally

While nutrition forms the foundation, strength training is the catalyst for metabolic health. Regular weight lifting increases muscle mass, which in turn raises your metabolic rate. This becomes increasingly important during perimenopause when maintaining muscle mass requires more intentional effort. The benefits extend beyond metabolism – strength training supports bone density, reduces anxiety through the release of endorphins, and improves insulin sensitivity.

A New Approach to Nourishment

It's time to reject the diet culture that promotes restriction and embrace a nourishing approach to eating. I advocate for focusing on adding, rather than subtracting, more protein, more fiber, more nutrient-dense foods. This isn't about following rigid rules; it's about creating a sustainable approach to eating that supports your body's changing needs.

Remember, the goal isn't just to survive perimenopause – it's to thrive through it. By properly fueling your body with adequate protein and fiber, supporting your nervous system through proper nutrition, and maintaining strength through regular exercise, you're not just managing symptoms – you're building a foundation for long-term health and vitality.

Start small: focus on adding protein to each meal, incorporating diverse fiber sources, and committing to regular strength training. Your body will thank you with more energy, better mood stability, and increased resilience during this transformative time.

CONNECT WITH ELIZABETH

www.strongchoices.com
www.instagram.com/strongchoices1
www.tiktok.com/@strongchoices

FROM ROCK BOTTOM TO PURPOSE: 5 STEPS TO TRANSFORM YOUR LIFE IN 2025

by Danger Foley

I'm Danger Foley—a DJ, music producer, and founder of The Danger Den, a sanctuary for high-impact artists to reconnect with themselves, their craft, and their fans. But before I became the person I am today, I was at rock bottom. A car accident left me in chronic pain, a career shift uprooted my stability and I lost a friend to suicide--all while my own mental health was spiraling. DJing started as a form of self-care, and from there, I discovered tools and practices that not only transformed my life but became the foundation for the space I dreamed of creating. The Danger Den is that space, but the lessons I've learned apply to anyone searching for alignment.

5 Steps to Change Your Life in 2025

1. Get to Know Yourself at Your Core
When you're at rock bottom, it's easy to want to escape the discomfort. But I leaned into it instead. Guided meditations and theta wave regression therapy helped me confront my shadows—the stories and blocks I picked up in childhood that were still holding me back. Facing those truths allowed me to rewrite them, to love the messy parts of myself, and to show up more authentically in the world. My favorite is tobemagnetic.com

2. Identify Your 5 Pillars of Truth
Once I understood myself more deeply, I created my 5 pillars of truth—values that I could anchor to when life felt chaotic. These pillars guided me to my ikigai, the Japanese concept for purpose. It's the sweet spot where what you love, what you're good at, what the world needs, and what can financially sustain you all intersect. For me, this became The Danger Den. With my experience in artist hospitality, sales, music and event production, I realized how much I enjoy hosting, music and mental health. I found a way to incorporate those things in a way that supported my 5 pillars and here we are.

3. Set Boundaries That Honor Your Growth
One of the hardest lessons I've learned is that not everyone is meant to come with you for the whole ride. As we grow, it's important to look around at the people we spend the most time with and ask ourselves the hard questions:

Do they inspire me? Do I like who I am around them? If the answer is no, what are we doing here? I also sought out expanders—people who embodied the life and energy I wanted to cultivate. I found that when I stopped trying to pull people along with me and instead run faster to join those already on my path, my life began to flow in a whole new way.

4. Make Therapy Non-Negotiable
Therapy was a game changer for me. It gave me the tools to break old patterns and see my blind spots. Having an unbiased, professional third party who can guide you through the hard parts of life--WHY is there stigma around this?! My partner and I even started couples counseling early in our relationship, not because anything was wrong, but to build a foundation for when things got hard. That proactive approach has been invaluable. The same goes for individual therapy—it's a space to hold yourself accountable, to heal, and to grow. Starting when life feels good makes it so much easier to weather the storms.

5. Create for the Sake of Creating
Art is healing, but not when it's tied to external validation like social media likes. Disconnect from instant dopamine hits and create for yourself. Whether it's music, painting, knitting or journaling, find a way to express yourself without judgment or pressure.

6. *bonus tip* Sauna/Cold Plunge: If you're able to do contrast therapy, even once a week, it can significantly help with not only fat loss and detoxification, but is also life changing for stress regulation and mental clarity.

These practices didn't just pull me out of rock bottom—they've expanded my consciousness, empathy and drive to the point where I want to shout them from the rooftops. I wouldn't be who or where I am today without these tips.

CONNECT WITH DANGER

www.dangerfoleymusic.com
@dangerfoleymusic
@dangerdenco

FENIX TV

SHE RISES
STUDIOS

EMPOWER**HER**
VIRTUAL SUMMIT 2025

When: January 23-25, 2025
Where: Exclusively on FENIX TV
Tickets: $49.97

Be part of the EmpowerHER Virtual Summit 2025, a transformative 3-day event designed to empower women entrepreneurs! Hosted by She Rises Studios, this summit features 50+ expert speakers sharing strategies, stories, and tools to help you break barriers, grow your business, and lead with confidence.

Why Watch?

- Access powerful insights from top women leaders.
- Learn strategies to grow your business and achieve success.
- Be part of a global movement supporting women entrepreneurs.

DON'T MISS OUT—GRAB YOUR TICKET NOW AND IGNITE YOUR SUCCESS!

A FRESH START:
OVERCOMING MENTAL BARRIERS AND EMBRACING CHANGE

by Anand Mehta, Executive Director at AMFM Healthcare

Embrace the Power of Change

The beginning of a new year often inspires us to reflect on the past and make resolutions for a fresh start. However, for many, the idea of change brings mental barriers that can be challenging to overcome. Whether it's fear of failure, self-doubt, or old habits, these obstacles can stand in the way of personal growth and transformation.

In this article, we will explore strategies to break through these mental barriers and embrace the changes that can lead to a year filled with vitality and well-being. Drawing from real-life examples, research, and practical advice, we'll help you take the first step toward a brighter future.

Understanding Mental Barriers: What Holds Us Back?

Mental barriers are psychological obstacles that prevent us from reaching our full potential. These can include:

- **Fear of failure**: The fear of not succeeding can paralyze us, making it difficult to take action.
- **Negative self-talk**: Constantly doubting your abilities can prevent you from trying new things.
- **Past experiences**: Traumatic or failed experiences can create a mental block that makes change feel impossible.
- **Perfectionism**: The belief that everything must be perfect before taking action can prevent progress.

Studies show that around 82% of people experience imposter syndrome or self-doubt, especially when attempting to make significant changes. Recognizing these mental barriers is the first step in breaking through them and making progress.

Strategies for Overcoming Mental Barriers

1. Shift Your Mindset: From Limiting Beliefs to Empowering Thoughts
One of the most effective ways to overcome mental barriers is to change how you view yourself and your abilities. This starts with shifting from a fixed mindset, which believes talents are innate, to a growth mindset, which embraces challenges as opportunities for growth.

Tips for shifting your mindset:

- **Practice positive affirmations**: Replace negative thoughts with empowering statements like, *"I am capable of growth,"* or *"I am capable of change."*
- **Focus on progress, not perfection**: Celebrate small victories, and remember that every step forward counts.

kelpHR

AFFIRMATIONS YOU CAN REPEAT DAILY

I believe in myself

I am limitless. Anything is possible

I am grateful for the life I have

I accept myself as I am

I am loved and admired everyday

Today is a new beginning

2. Set Realistic Goals: Start Small

Often, the idea of making a dramatic change can feel overwhelming. Instead of setting large, unattainable goals, focus on smaller, manageable tasks that build toward your bigger vision. Breaking down goals into bite-sized pieces helps maintain motivation and reduces the pressure of perfection.

Actionable steps:

- Set specific, measurable, attainable, relevant, and time-bound (SMART) goals.
- Start with micro-goals: For example, instead of aiming to *"get fit,"* start by committing to a 10-minute walk each day.

SET MICRO-GOALS

BIG GOALS	MICRO-GOALS
Get in shape	Walk around the block during your lunch break
Read 25 books	Read for 5-minutes before bed
Save for a home	Transfer $1-5 dollars to savings daily
Be more productive	Finish one to-do list task each day
Become a JavaScript expert	Do one coding exercise

3. Overcome Self-Doubt: Build Confidence Through Action

Self-doubt can prevent us from making progress. One effective way to counteract this is by building confidence through action. Taking small steps toward your goals builds momentum and gradually reduces fear and doubt.

Example: Take the story of Sarah, a woman who struggled with anxiety and fear of failure. She set a goal to change careers, but her self-doubt kept holding her back. By breaking down the process into smaller tasks—updating her resume, researching new careers, and attending networking events—she gradually built the confidence she needed to make the leap. Today, she works in a field she loves, all because she took action despite her doubts.

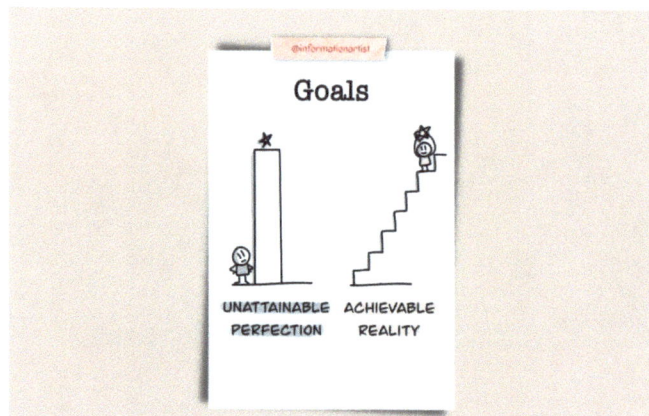

@informationartist

Goals

UNATTAINABLE PERFECTION   ACHIEVABLE REALITY

4. Practice Self-Compassion: Be Kind to Yourself

Being overly critical of ourselves can create more mental barriers. Practicing self-compassion—being kind and understanding when we experience setbacks—helps to remove the shame and guilt that can hinder progress.

Tips for practicing self-compassion:
- **Acknowledge your feelings**: Instead of judging yourself for feeling anxious or fearful, recognize it as part of the process.
- **Treat yourself like a friend**: When you make mistakes, offer yourself the same kindness you would to a close friend.

5. Visualize Success: Imagine the Future You Want

Visualization is a powerful tool that can help you overcome mental barriers. By mentally rehearsing your success, you can reduce anxiety and boost motivation.

How to visualize success:
- **Create a mental image of your desired outcome**: See yourself achieving your goals, whether it's running a marathon, landing a new job, or improving your mental health.
- **Feel the emotions of success**: Imagine the pride, happiness, and satisfaction of having overcome your barriers.

Your Fresh Start Awaits

Overcoming mental barriers and embracing change is not an overnight process, but with determination, self-compassion, and a positive mindset, it is entirely possible. By breaking your goals into smaller steps, building confidence through action, and practicing kindness to yourself, you can create a fresh start for the year ahead.

Remember, change is not easy, but it is worth the effort. Whether you are looking to improve your career, your relationships, or your mental well-being, the first step is always the hardest. However, each small step you take will lead you closer to the life you want to create.

FAQs

Q: How can I start overcoming mental barriers?
A: Start by identifying the specific barriers that are holding you back, such as fear of failure or negative self-talk. From there, work on shifting your mindset, setting small, achievable goals, and practicing self-compassion.

Q: Is it normal to feel resistant to change?
A: Yes, resistance to change is a natural part of the process. Embrace the discomfort, as it is often a sign that you are pushing beyond your comfort zone and growing.

Q: Can visualization really help me overcome mental barriers?
A: Yes, visualization can be a powerful tool. By imagining success, you can reduce anxiety and boost your confidence, making it easier to take the necessary steps toward achieving your goals.

CONNECT WITH ANAND

www.linkedin.com/in/anand-mehta-lmft-094a4b93
www.amfmtreatment.com

she wins

A Fresh START FOR January

Written by Hanna Olivas - CEO of She Rises Studios & FENIX TV

A new year dawns, crisp and bright,
With dreams that dance in winter's light.
January whispers, "Begin again,"
A time to rise, to grow, to mend.
In the chill of morning, she finds her way,
With resolve as steady as each new day.
The past year's struggles, she lets them go,
For She Wins by choosing the path to grow.
She knows that kindness is power, true,
That nice girls finish first in all they pursue.
She greets each morning with strength anew,
Ready to face what she must push through.
Others may rush, may scheme, may strive,
But she knows her way to truly thrive.
For the heart that lifts, that shares, that cares,
Finds joy and purpose everywhere.
With open hands and a hopeful heart,
She builds her world, a work of art.
Every act of kindness, a seed to sow,
As she steps into her year, aglow.
January stands, a clean, white page,
Ready to carry her through each stage.
And with each step, her light grows bright,
For She Wins by shining kindness's light.
So here's to fresh starts, to brave, bold dreams,
To kindness sown in winter streams.
Let the year unfold with love in view—
For nice girls finish first, and so will you.

#SheWins #NiceGirlsFinishFirst

www.sherisesstudios.com

NUTRITION FOR VITALTY: FUELING YOUR BODY FOR ENERGY, LONGEVITY, AND WELL-BEING

by Catherine Gervacio

Everyone knows that fueling yourself with the right nutrients is very important to keep your energy levels high, your body strong, and your mind sharp. That's why foods rich in vitamins, minerals, antioxidants, and healthy macronutrients are your secret weapons to vitality and well-being. Here's how to build a diet that nourishes and energizes you for the long haul.

What Are Nutrient-Dense Foods?
Nutrient-dense foods are rich in vitamins, minerals, and other essential nutrients for the calories they contain. Examples are fruits, leafy greens, lean proteins, whole grains, and healthy fats. These foods not only sustain your energy but also reduce the risk of chronic diseases and slow down the aging process.

Why Nutrient Density Matters
A 2023 study published in Food Science & Nutrition shows that functional foods with high antioxidant potential can provide an effective, affordable approach to managing diseases associated with free radicals while minimizing the toxicities and side effects often associated with conventional medications.

Another study found that consuming high-nutrient foods enhances energy levels and cognition, helping people feel more alert and less fatigued. The science is clear on this. What you eat directly affects how you feel today and how healthy you'll be tomorrow.

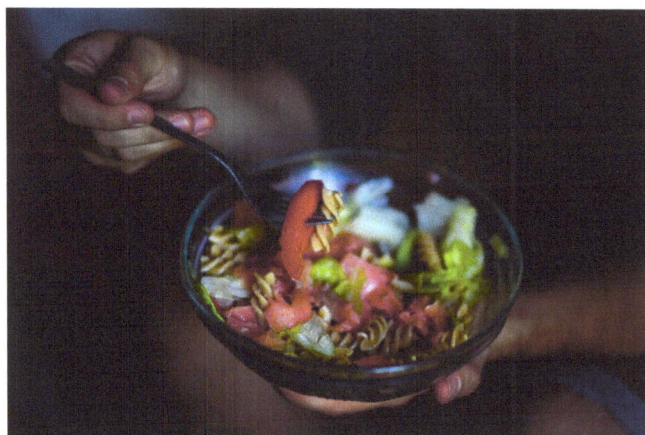

Essential Nutrient-Dense Foods
1. Leafy Greens
Spinach, kale, and Swiss chard are rich in vitamins A, C, and K, and they're also high in fiber. Add them to smoothies, salads, or sautés to boost your nutrient intake effortlessly.
2. Berries
Blueberries, raspberries, and strawberries are rich in antioxidants. They protect your cells from damage and support brain health. Top them on yogurt or oatmeal for a refreshing snack.
3. Lean Proteins
Chicken, turkey, fish, and plant-based options like tofu and lentils supply essential amino acids for muscle repair and energy production. Balance your plate with protein for sustained vitality.
4. Whole Grains
Quinoa, oats, and brown rice are high in fiber and B vitamins, stabilizing blood sugar levels and keeping energy steady throughout the day.
5. Healthy Fats
Avocados, nuts, seeds, and olive oil provide omega-3 fatty acids and other healthy fats that promote heart and brain health. Sprinkle seeds on salads or blend avocado into a creamy dressing.
6. Superfoods
Include spirulina, chia seeds, and turmeric for an extra nutrient boost. These foods are known for their anti-inflammatory and energy-boosting properties.

Tips to Make Nutrient-Dense Eating Easy
1. **Plan Your Meals:** Prepping your meals ahead of time ensures you always have healthy options whatever happens.
2. **Balance Your Plate:** The plate method divides your plate into three sections: half for non-starchy vegetables (e.g., broccoli, spinach), a quarter for lean proteins (e.g., chicken, tofu), and a quarter for whole grains or starchy foods (e.g., brown rice, sweet potatoes). Add a small portion of healthy fats and a drink like water.
3. **Snack Smart:** Replace chips and candy with nuts, fruit, or veggie sticks with hummus.
4. **Stay Hydrated:** Drink plenty of water and try adding lemon or cucumber slices for flavor.

How to Build a Day of Nutrient-Dense Eating
- **Breakfast**: A smoothie with spinach, banana, frozen berries, and almond milk.
- **Snack**: A handful of nuts and an apple.
- **Lunch**: Grilled salmon with sweet potatoes and steamed broccoli.
- **Snack**: Carrot sticks with hummus.
- **Dinner**: Turkey stir-fry with brown rice and mixed vegetables.
- **Dessert**: Greek yogurt with a drizzle of honey and chia seeds.

A Year of Vitality Awaits
Small, consistent changes in your diet can transform your energy and health. So, stock your kitchen with wholesome options, experiment with recipes, and prioritize fueling your body with the best nature has to offer.

CONNECT WITH CATHERINE
www.living.fit/pages/catherine-gervacio

FROM TRAUMA TO TRIUMPH: A JOURNEY TO EMPOWERMENT AND HEALING

By Trina Kennedy RSW, BAHSA

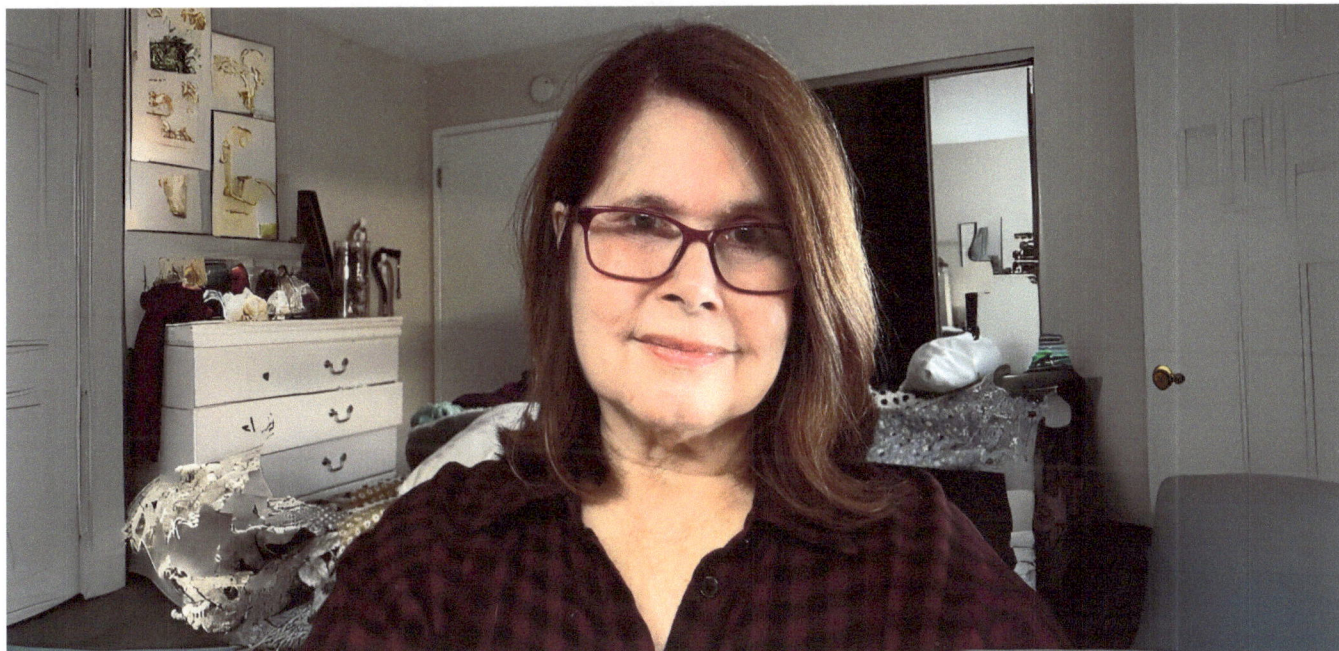

My vision is to create a global community where individuals are empowered with the tools to foster self-regulation, enhance their well-being, and embark on transformative healing journeys. This vision fills me with excitement, gratitude, and yes—a bit of fear. Growth often requires stepping into discomfort, and I am embracing this challenge.

At 16, I faced some of the darkest moments of my life. I felt alone and overwhelmed by hopelessness, despair, and pain. In that darkness, I took actions that were desperate cries for help. Thankfully, I found a lifeline in a remarkable therapist named Joan. She made me feel seen, heard, and safe for the first time in my life. Without judgment or trying to fix me, she held space for me to begin the healing process—a journey I continue today.

Joan's impact inspired my life's work. I knew I wanted to offer others the same transformative experience she had given me. Nearly 30 years ago, I began my career in human services, walking alongside countless individuals as they navigated their healing journeys. My hope has always been to create a space of safety, compassion, and possibility, just as Joan did for me. This work revealed my true purpose: to teach, guide, and nurture growth and insight in others. Few things are as rewarding as witnessing someone experience an *"aha"* moment when they connect the dots and realize their potential.

Sharing my experiences and knowledge to empower others has become my greatest passion. I believe in divine timing, and I know I am exactly where I need to be to make an impact—not just one-on-one, but on a much larger scale.

That belief is what inspired me to write my book, From Trauma to Triumph and What Lies Between. It combines my personal story with cutting-edge research to inspire readers to face their trauma, recognize their resilience, and celebrate their triumphs. Writing this book has been exhilarating and humbling. Dreaming big is thrilling, even when it's scary.

We don't grow by staying in our comfort zones. Transformation happens when we push through fear to discover the life-changing possibilities on the other side.

As I look at all I've accomplished and what lies ahead, I feel immense gratitude. My career and life are rooted in service, and I'm passionate about sharing what I've learned. Whether through my book, workshops, or coaching, my mission remains the same: to help others heal, grow, and step into their greatness.
If my 16-year-old self could see me now, she'd know the pain wasn't the end of the story—it was the beginning of a journey from trauma to triumph.

CONNECT WITH TRINA

www.linkedin.com/in/trinakennedy
@trinalkennedy
www.facebook.com/trinaleekennedy
www. trinaleekennedy.ca

LET'S CELEBRATE

AT THE HEART OF VITALITY

by DK Hillard

Vitality, the presence of our whole life force, is greater than physical health alone. We tend to live in our minds, operating as if the control center there is in charge of all of our choices and actions. In truth, the mind is not capable of running the show that we call our lives. It operates on ego, belief systems and programming, like a computer. Without the spiritual component, it tends to run amok. The mind is best used in service to the soul, not in charge of it.

Our mind knows facts, processes input and makes decisions that are often based on fear. I'm referring to all the ego-driven thoughts that tell us who we should be, how we should act, and what our lives are supposed to look like, all designed to be liked, accepted by others and keep us safe.

Our heart tells a different story. It bases its choices on love, passion, and our soul's truth. We are not computers. We are human beings who were designed with emotions for a reason. When we follow our hearts, not blindly, but from knowing our truth and trusting ourselves, we are perfectly guided.

The basis of Shamanism, the spiritual path I have been following for a good part of my life, is the interconnectivity of all things. Natural forces, the elements of our earth, and the heavens—all are thought of as family. Everything has a soul, permeated with essence and consciousness and deserves our reverence. Our work is to find our own soul essence and in doing so, our true power.

We interact with the spirit world to gain information and guidance, often leading to healing of some sort, be it physical, emotional, or spiritual. In truth they are all connected. Healing often comes in subtle ways and not in the time frame we wish.

Being fully vital and alive requires the presence of your soul essence, your power. We need to remember who we truly are and often some guidance is helpful. When we are not living our truth, even success on a worldly stage can leave us feeling empty. The quest for truth can lead to a life of fulfillment and meaning beyond imagination. A life without it, pales in comparison, though on the surface it might appear all glittery and gold.

I have been strongly guided to offer my gifts as agents of healing. I do this through sacred ceremony and journeys to the spirit world which inform how and what I create for both myself and others. My creative path for decades was my personal healing journey, each image, a message from Spirit to help me find my way back to my true self. I walked this path for decades and experienced the hardship of loss on many levels before I was ready to be whole again. It is not an easy path, but to be a vehicle for healing I had to walk the walk first.

I can't remember a time in my life when I followed a given path. Forging my own, creating my own niche, honing my gifts in unconventional ways, has been my experience. I have found that not fitting in, difficult as that was at times, has been a tremendous advantage in creating my work and my life. I have had to find my own way and as a result, what I offer others is unlike anything else. I am not a traditional artist, Shaman or healer. I have experience, wisdom and mastery in certain areas that I can now offer in a unique way to help others find their true essence.

Every painting, each poem I've written, and most of my writing until recently has been Spirit's way of sending me breadcrumbs to follow so that I could be wholly myself and stand in my truth. That has freed me to share my discoveries and offer guidance as you walk your own path. There is no greater fulfillment than sharing the jewels of my journey.

The work I do now was born out of my desire to experience bliss and abundance, not just for a moment, but as a way of life. After years of hardship, illness and loss, I knew I was ready to receive more. Surrounding myself with things that delight my senses reminds me of the abundance I can receive when I am willing to open the door. And the same is true for all of us. Mother Earth is not lacking in treasure. We must be open to receiving it, to seeing the magic around us and to allowing ourselves to experience it through all of our senses. That is the beauty of being human: we feel.

Physical sensation provides access to a deeper experience of yourself and to a path that transcends the mind and transports you beyond the present. The feeling of bliss when we are touched in just the right way expands our energy, connecting us to our natural state of love, compassion and joy—we can feel the opening of our hearts. Some call this rapture.

I knew that I needed to translate my visions into a rapturous experience for myself. I needed to feel that energy with all of my senses. In the process, I have discovered that others feel it as well. My art has become more than a way to heal myself and bring myself back to who I truly am. It has transformed into a healing tool to facilitate a connection through your body to your soul, a way of remembering who you truly are.

It has become medicine for your body and soul.

CONNECT WITH DK

www.facebook.com/dkhillardart
www.instagram.com/dkhillard
www.youtube.com/@dkhillard
www.dkhillard.com
www.dkhillardart.com

MIND YOUR MINDFULNESS

by Jerry Brook

Lately many people seem to be speaking about *"Mindfulness,"* but what is it they are talking about? Is this pure hooey or is there a real and practical side to this?

We need to define our terms. Proper, meaningful communication requires clarity and specification. It isn't helpful to discuss a topic or subject if
a) we don't know what it is that is being discussed or
b) we simply don't understand what is meant by the words that are being chosen to be used.

Mindfulness, as the name implies, involves the mind. It is therefore a thought process. The act of being mindful consists of being aware. But being aware of what exactly? It is about being aware of a situation or circumstance and is literally situational awareness both in the present as well as for likely future events. Like any game of strategy, we must consider the immediate context, while at the same time anticipating the next probable action.

In addition to being aware of the *"what,"* mindfulness must also include being aware of the *"who."* We need to be aware and mindful of ourselves and our actions. At the same time we must realize that our actions are being influenced and or influencing the actions of others.

However, it doesn't end there. After all, what would be the point of simply being aware and not taking any action meant to either contribute to or detract from the impending situation or circumstance?

In order to fulfill the essence of Mindfulness we must also be conscientious. So, what does it mean to be conscientious? Conscientiousness is the focus and attention to detail that is given to the principles that we value and believe in. The more we care about something, the more thoughtful we are about that ideal. The act of being conscientious is the mechanism by which we express our commitment to the situation and to those who are being, or will be, affected by it.

In other words, mindfulness is the operation of being aware and acting in an intentional manner on that knowledge. Simply put, mindfulness is clearly not pseudo-science. It is grounded in our ability to comprehend our surroundings as well as our desire to concentrate our attention on the things that we value.

What mindfulness is not:
People apply the incorrect adage, *"Do unto others as you would have them do unto you."* This is a self-centered view of the world in which we live. It assumes that all other people are exactly as we are and want only those things that we want. Nothing could be further from the truth. It makes no sense to give someone strawberry ice cream only because we happen to prefer strawberry ice cream.

Instead, we must determine whether the other person, first even likes ice cream, second what flavor do they prefer, and lastly do they even want any ice cream at this particular time? In other words, *"Do unto others as they wish done unto them, within the limits of what it is that we are willing to do."*

The Relationship Building Game!

Build and maintain better relationships
While having fun doing it.

goodtogether

Available Both On

App Store
Google Play

Also, Don't forget yourself in the overall equation. There are those things that others may desire that are either beyond our control, or not aligned with our values and beliefs. We aren't supporting others when we aren't supporting ourselves. Those that have no values have no value.

Now that we have that out of the way and we are all on the same page, how do we do it? That is, how do we practice mindfulness? Can mindfulness be learned?

Because mindfulness and by extension conscientiousness can be traced to mental and physical processes, they can in turn be learned, improved, and extended. Just as we can get better at games of strategy with practice, we can become even more mindful.

We begin by avoiding distractions. We need to be present and in the moment. You can't see what is going on around you, even under your very nose, if that nose is buried in your phone. First, we look with our eyes and then we look with our minds.

Next, we must ask questions. Imagine the situation in all of its probabilities from the perspectives of all of the various parties in that circumstance. That is, put yourself in the shoes of all of the other players. Ask yourself, what is it that they are seeing, how is it that they are feeling? If the tables were turned, how would I react?

From there we must decide on the appropriate course of action. This is a simple Cost Benefit Analysis. What is the cost and what are the benefits?

Applying these principles properly and consistently are the keys to learning how to be a more reliable and amenable person. In order to assist others in their quest for healthy relationships I have created an app just for the purpose of being present and learning more about what others are thinking or going through. My app, The Good Together Game, fosters mindfulness in a way that is easy for the players to utilize.

About Good Together App

The *"Good Together"* App was created to help people strengthen their personal and professional relationship through fun, personalized interactions. It was created by Author and Relationship Guru Jerry Brook. Jerry fuses his relationship experience with a background in analytics to help others maintain better relationships. As an Industrial Computer Controls Specialist, Jerry's experience in problem solving and analytical thinking inspired him to look at relationships in a similar way. In addition, he also draws on his own personal relationships to offer practical, intelligent, and sometimes funny relationship stories and advice. He currently lives in Houston, Texas. Learn more at **www.goodtogether.com** and **www.JerryBrook.com.**

THE GIFT OF YOGA:
MAKING YOGA ACCESSIBLE

by Buffy Olson

The country has and has been experiencing an obesity epidemic; the CDC reports that in 2023 35% of the population has obesity (CDC Newsroom, 2024). The CDC lists the reasons for obesity to high levels of stress, lack of access to healthy food, poor sleep, and safe places to be active (2024). The CDC further states that obesity prevention and healthy weight family programs are necessary to bettering the health of our community and individuals.

Yoga serves as not only a strategy preventative to obesity related to health ailments, but also a treatment. Yoga has been related to easing anxiety, depression, stress, weight management, and improved immunity and overall improved feelings of well-being. The benefits of yoga are so numerous that Mr. Sengupta says that "The holistic science of yoga is the best method for prevention as well as management of stress and stress-induced disorders (2024)." Obesity and stress related disorders are strongly connected with poverty.

The APA states that health disparities, which include obesity and stress-related illnesses, often stem from economic detriments including poorer education and geographical locations (n.d.) and lower socio-economic status. Unfortunately, many people do not have safe access to yoga studios or spaces that they feel safe practicing yoga or have a lack of knowledge of how to get started in their own practice. There is no one way or place to practice yoga; yoga doesn't need to exist only in boutiques or gyms where memberships are often inaccessible for certain economic groups that suffer from obesity and stress. There are places and platforms that make yoga accessible, for example local recreation centers and YouTube, but yoga needs to be made more accessible for all people, and awareness brought to all of the health benefits of practicing yoga regularly to communities that need it most; yoga should be in our schools taught to our children and teachers, yoga should be made accessible to our truckers, laborers, and the many different groups of our working class.

Research on the exact benefits of practicing yoga is still being done but there has been enough to know for certain that regular yoga practice increases not only quality of life, but it also increases lifespan.

All of us in the health and wellness fields of work whether it's mental health, physical fitness, or the medical field must work to educate our communities and make yoga and yoga tools more accessible for all people with particular care for those who are working in public service, labor jobs, and lower income. We need more yoga accessibility not only for a better society today but for a much healthier future.

American Psychological Association. (n.d.). Fact sheet: Health disparities and stress. American Psychological Association. www.apa.org/topics/racism-bias-discrimination/health-disparities-stress

New CDC Data Show Adult Obesity Prevalence Remains High. CDC Newsroom. (2024, September 12). www.cdc.gov/media/releases/2024/p0912-adult-obesity.html

Sengupta P. (2012). Health Impacts of Yoga and Pranayama: A State-of-the-Art Review. International journal of preventive medicine, 3(7), 444–458.

CONNECT WITH BUFFY

www.Firevinyasa.com (coming soon)
www.tiktok.com/@olsonbuffy
www.youtube.com/@firevinyasabybuffy
www.facebook.com/share/1HRQiXXFPE

HOW TO PRIORITIZE NUTRITION, HEALTH AND WELLBEING IN 2025 AS AN ATHLETE

by Marina Paul, SPRHRA Founder

To kick things off...

I don't believe I will ever overcome mental health issues. Same thing with eating disorders, both have left scars. I can't deny that thoughts don't come up, especially in a world where specific looks and body types are constantly bombarding us. The most helpful thing I did to work through my eating disorders and mental health issues was to uncover the root of the issue, which was that I just didn't like myself. I thought I wasn't good enough because I thought differently, expressed myself differently, was super intense, and pretty goofy. I cared so much about fitting in, that I thought I needed to change who I was, specifically physically, to do that. When I changed my mindset, and started doing the things I wanted to do and being the way I wanted to, I started to heal. This took 8 years, and I'm still doing the work!

Contrary to a lot of the advice on what to eat, how to workout, when to wake up... I really believe you have to figure out what works best for you. I believe we are all one of one. I think the best thing you can do is eliminate the things that feel most unnatural. Challenging is good, but unnatural, I don't think will lead to a sustainable, fun lifestyle. Think of it like playing a sport or an instrument. I am not naturally good at instruments, but I am naturally good at sports, and I love sports. So I build a lifestyle to what's conducive to what I'm good at, what I love and that together makes me feel really good.

We build our clothing with the mindset that health starts from the outside in. Our brains pick up the sensations on our bodies, so if something doesn't feel good on the outside, we're going to think something's wrong with us. Women think that if clothing doesn't fit, it's their fault. This is so wrong!

We try to build our clothing to feel incredible on your skin, no matter the size and shape of your body. We don't ever get this right the first time, which is why we constantly test and garner feedback from elite college and pro athletes as well as high school and youth athletes. Most importantly, we want women to know that it's the clothes, it's not them.

Athletes are really good at being told what to do and executing, but I think we struggle when we have to coach ourselves. If you need a coach, go find one and explain what you think your goals are. Also, sometimes our goal is really a symptom. For example, "I want a faster time." We don't know how to get there or why we might not be running as fast as we could. Maybe a faster time isn't the goal, then. Maybe the goal is getting your pelvis in the right position, so that you can run faster. The point is, as driven and strong-headed athletes, we also have to be flexible to life's game :)

For 2025, my goals are specific to my body, so I would definitely recommend figuring out what your body needs! This structure is no different from when I was a competitive athlete because being an entrepreneur is so similar. Here are the areas I assess for building out my goals:

- How much and how well do you sleep?
- How do you eat?
- What do you do when you wake up?
- What do you ingest (food, shows & media, etc.)?
- When do you look at your phone?
- What do you do before bed?
- I would also look into Postural Restoration and breathwork. I've found that calming my nervous system has been some of the most beneficial work I've done.

CONNECT WITH MARINA

www.sprhra.com
*www.instagram.com/sprhra_*
www.amazon.com/Becoming-Superhero-Awaken-Superpowers-Inspire/dp/1636768563

CHECK OUT THESE AVAILABLE BOOKS ON AMAZON

THE PERFECT NEW YEARS GIFT!

PUBLISHED BY SHE RISES STUDIOS

Books make timeless gifts, offering stories, inspiration, and a touch of magic. From heartwarming novels to motivational reads and beautifully illustrated coffee table books, there's something for everyone. Give the gift of imagination and joy this Christmas!

amazon

SHE RISES
STUDIOS

THE PERFECT NEW YEARS GIFT!

SUMMONING THE GOWL-DIE

Henry Cline

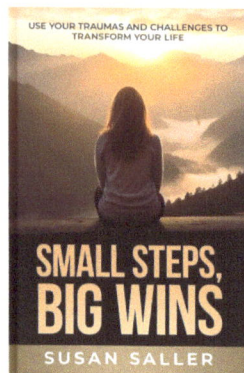

SMALL STEPS, BIG WINS

Susan Saller

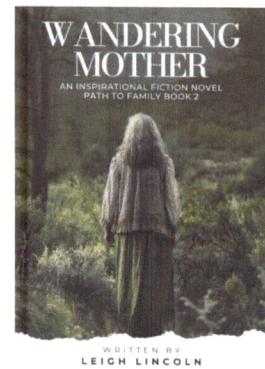

WANDERING MOTHER

Leigh Lincoln

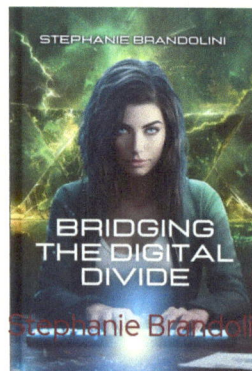

BRIDGING THE DIGITAL DIVIDE

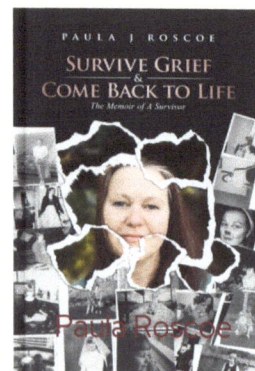

Stephanie Brandolini

SURVIVING GRIEF & COME BACK TO LIFE

Paula Roscoe

amazon

SHE RISES
STUDIOS

THE PERFECT NEW YEARS GIFT!

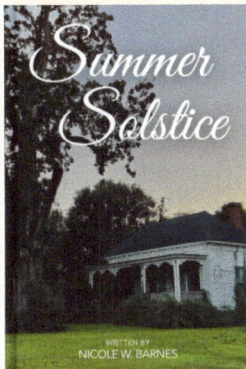

SUMMER SOLSTICE

Henry Cline

CHANGE FOR GOOD: THE TRANSFORMATIVE POWER OF GIVING AS THE ULITMATE TOOL

Susan Saller

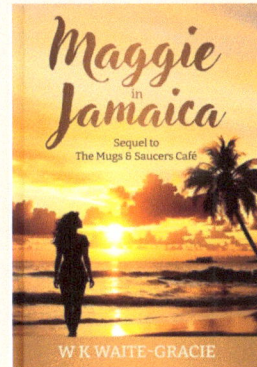

MAGGIE IN JAMAICA

Katherine-Waite Gracie

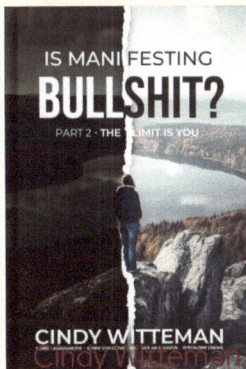

IS MANIFESTING BULLSHIT: PART 2

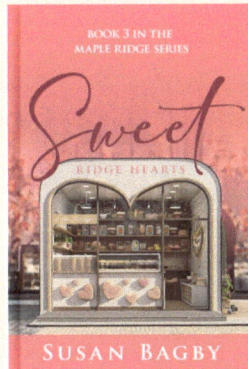

SWEET RIDGE HEART

Susan Bagby
(SP Author)

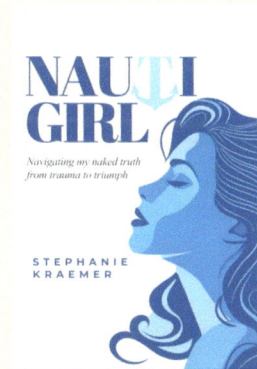

NAUTI GIRL

Stephanie Pavletich-Kraemer

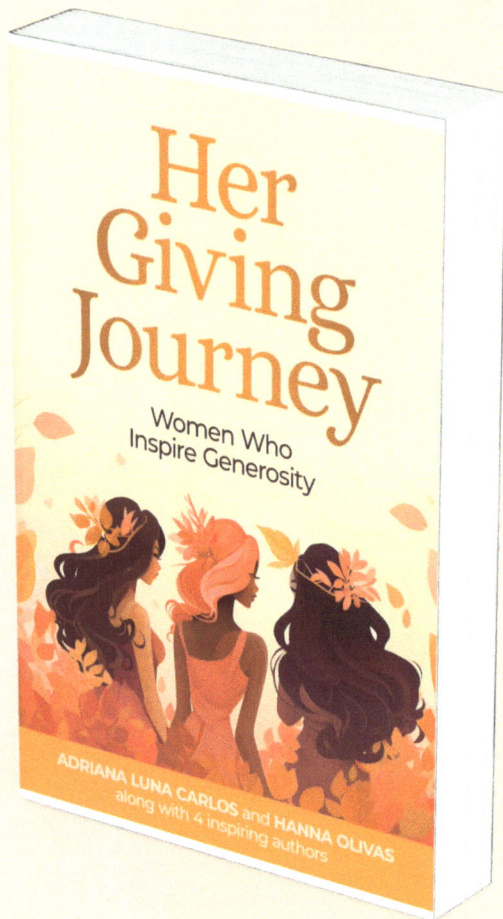

THE PERFECT NEW YEARS GIFT!

Her Giving Journey: Women Who Inspire Generosity celebrates extraordinary women whose acts of kindness have sparked meaningful change in their communities and beyond. This inspiring collection features local heroes and global changemakers who used creativity, courage, and compassion to overcome challenges and uplift others.

Through their powerful stories, you'll discover the boundless potential of generosity and reflect on your own capacity for kindness. Join **Adriana Luna Carlos, Hanna Olivas, and four inspiring co-authors—Jennifer Jonassaint, Dr. Sonya A. McKinzie, Krista Sobieski, and Karen Rudolf**—as they motivate you to embrace the spirit of giving and create a brighter, more compassionate future

**Her
Giving
Journey**
Women Who
Inspire Generosity

ADRIANA LUNA CARLOS and HANNA OLIVAS
along with 4 inspiring authors

SHOP NOW ON AMAZON

amazon

SHE RISES
STUDIOS

THE POWER OF PUBLISHING
WHY PUBLISH A BOOK, YOU ASK?

Publishing a book is one of the most fulfilling ways to share your story with the world and leave a lasting legacy. It boosts your credibility and highlights your expertise in your industry. Plus, you'll be stepping into the massive $138.5 billion book market industry —and it's still growing!

Best of all, it's easier now than ever before to get your book out there. How exciting is that?

At She Rises Studios, we are on a mission to become the top publishing house for women in the USA. We believe in the power of storytelling to create influencers and stronger communities. We're here to help you break barriers, grow, and make waves in the publishing world.

Get published with us TODAY!
Visit *www.SheRisesStudios.com* or email us at contact@sherisesstudios.com

LOVE YOUR LYMPH: SELF CARE PART 1

by Tina Quinn

Confession. The year was 2021. Even though I had been a nurse for 24 years, my knowledge of the lymphatic system was limited. Sure, I had oncology patients, some familiarity with lymph nodes, and some of my patients had lymphedema. In reality, I didn't know specifically how the lymphatic system worked.

I'm also a licensed massage therapist, so at the suggestion of health professionals, I enrolled in a 135-hour class to become a Certified Lymphedema Therapist (CLT), a foundational training. It made a positive impact on my health by helping me to identify my congested lymphatic areas. I recognized I was in the beginning stages of lymphedema due to standing during my long nursing shifts. This made my lymphatic training personal. My education has continued ever since.

In a nutshell, our lymphatic system is a network of tissues, organs, and vessels that helps the body fight infection, maintain fluid levels, and absorb fats. It includes our tonsils, thymus, spleen, and bone marrow. I like to think of it as a one-way highway system of lymph capillaries, lymph vessels, and lymph nodes that collect and remove cellular waste, toxins, inflammation, and cancer cells from our body. Sometimes our lymphatic highway encounters *"roadblocks."*

Signs Our Lymphatic System is Congested:
- Tiredness, brain fog, anxiety, mood swings
- Stiff, tight, aching, muscle or joint pain
- Swelling: fingers/ankles/feet/legs, puffy eyes/face, swelling in breasts before menses
- Allergies: stuffy and congested nose, sinus issues, swollen glands
- Skin issues: dry skin, acne, rash, itching, changes in skin texture (loss of elasticity, cellulite)
- Change in body composition: puffy and new "fatty" areas (abdomen, axilla, chin, medial knees, legs, around incisional areas)
- Digestive issues: new food sensitivities, bloating, stomach aches, constipation, difficulty losing weight, irregular bowel movements

After I see a client for a lymphatic drainage session, we discuss daily practices to keep our lymphatic system flowing. It truly makes an impact.

1. Movement Matters!
My clients experience positive changes when they add exercise, including decreased inflammation and swelling. When our muscles contract, our lymph is propelled through lymphatic capillaries and vessels. Without movement, lymph can become stagnant, and cellular debris and toxins can linger.

Prolonged sitting and standing can cause gravity-dependent swelling, and chronic swelling can contribute to the development of lymphedema.
- Introduce movement whenever possible to increase blood flow.
- Heel raises use our calf muscles and help prevent swelling.
- Consider wearing graduated compression socks to prevent swelling. There are fun patterns and colors to choose from.

2. Nutrition, Nutrition, Nutrition
Our lymphatic system transports approximately 8 to 12 liters of lymph fluid and protein daily. Unhealthy nutrition causes the liver to increase lymph production, which can overwhelm and exceed our lymphatic transport capacity.

Prioritize:
- Anti-inflammatory foods such as fruits, vegetables, omega-3 fatty acids, and herbs like turmeric and ginger reduce inflammation.
- Fiber promotes daily regular bowel movements, which helps eliminate toxins.
- Lean protein sources.
- Hydration supports proper lymph fluid movement.
- A healthy weight prevents pressure on the lymphatic system.

Avoid:
- Excess salt, which can lead to fluid retention.
- Refined sugars and processed food, which contribute to inflammation.
- Alcohol and caffeine, which can constrict blood vessels.
- Gluten-containing grains or dairy, which may trigger an immune response.

3. Sleep
Sleep helps our brain's glymphatic system to clear toxins.

4. Deep Breathing
Our body has 600–800 lymph nodes, approximately 200 of which are in our abdomen. When we inhale and exhale deeply, the rise and fall of our diaphragm help stimulate lymphatic flow.

Stay Tuned for Part 2
Part 2 will show a quick and easy routine to open up your lymphatic drainage. Stay tuned!

CONNECT WITH TINA

www.detroitmetrolymphaticmassage.com
Instagram: Detroit Metro Lymphatic Massage

Choose LIVING & DREAMING, Instead of Worrying & Wondering

STRUGGLING WITH BLOATING, FATIGUE, OR MYSTERIOUS HEALTH ISSUES?

Join **HEATHER HANSON**, a gut health expert and mindset coach, in her **DIGESTIVE CPR PROGRAM**.

Boost your energy, eliminate bloating, improve focus, gain confidence, and love your body again.

Scan the QR code to book a complimentary consultation.

SCAN ME

📞 512-762-4033   ✉ heatherhansonnutrition@gmail.com

🌐 www.flourishnutritionaltherapy.com

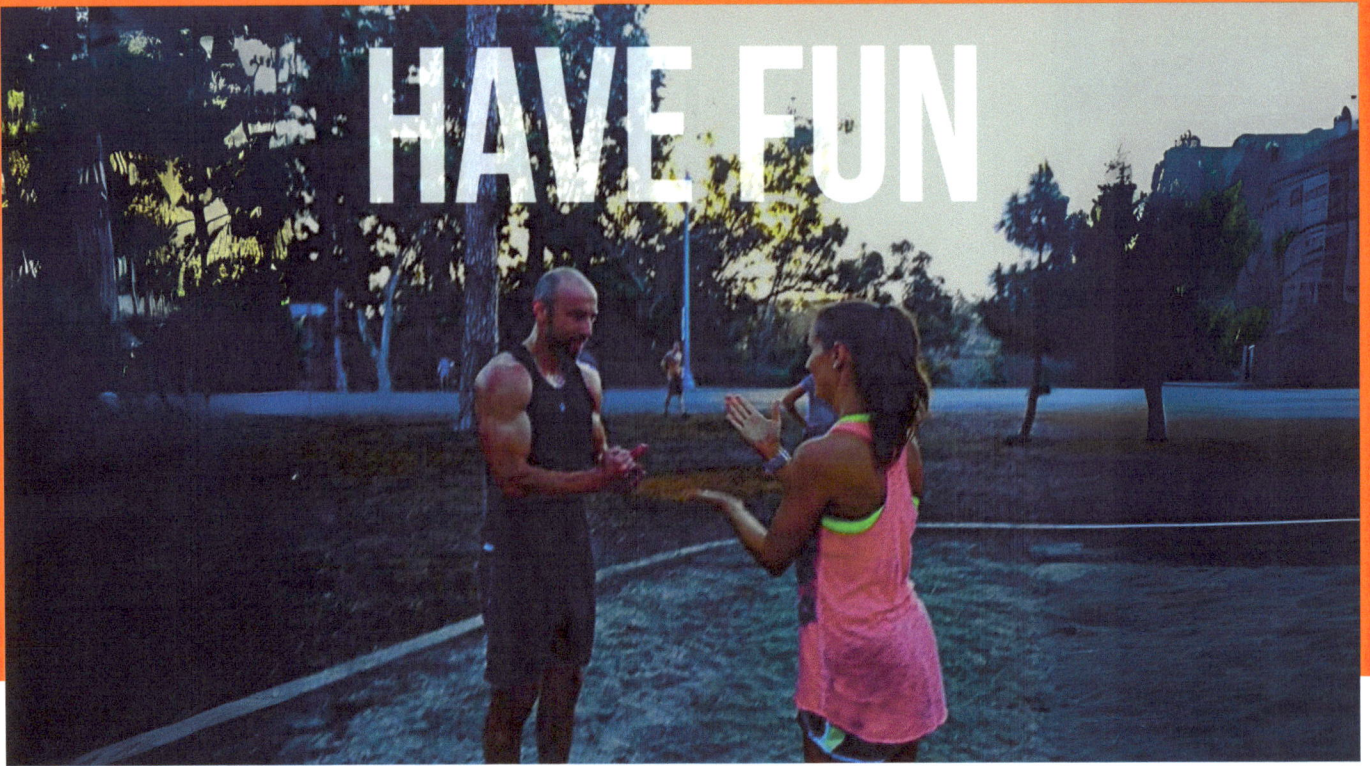

FITNESS ROUTINES FOR THE NEW YEAR: STARTING STRONG AND STAYING COMMITTED

By Justin Kraft
Founder and Personal Trainer at Aspire 2 More Fitness

The New Year brings a fresh slate, offering an ideal opportunity to kickstart your fitness journey. Whether your goal is to build muscle, lose weight, or improve overall health, a well-structured plan is key to starting strong and staying committed. This guide will help you set achievable goals, design effective routines, and maintain long-term motivation.

Setting the Foundation: Goals and Mindset
Goal Setting: The SMART Approach
To succeed in your fitness routines for the New Year, begin with clear, measurable objectives. The SMART method (Specific, Measurable, Achievable, Relevant, and Time-bound) can help.

- **Specific**: Define your goal (e.g., lose 15 pounds or bench press your body weight).
- **Measurable**: Track progress through metrics like the number of reps, weight lifted, or body fat percentage.
- **Achievable**: Start with realistic targets to avoid frustration (e.g., Increase ability to do 5 additional pushups in 2 weeks or run a 8 minute mile in a month)
- **Relevant**: Align your fitness goals with personal values, such as improving health or preparing for a competition.
- **Time-bound**: Set a deadline to create urgency and focus.

Develop a Positive Mindset
Fitness success requires mental commitment. Embrace progress over perfection and celebrate small victories, such as increasing the number of reps or mastering new exercises. You may find over time that you will begin to love the process over the result itself.

Building Your Fitness Routine
Start Small and Progress Gradually
Jumping into an intense workout plan can lead to burnout or injury. Start with manageable routines and gradually increase intensity. Make your routine fun and you will find that you will gain a general feeling of well being.

Week 1 Example:
- **Warm-Up**: 5 minutes of dynamic stretches or light cardio.
- **Strength Training**: 2 sets of 8-10 reps of bodyweight squats, push-ups, and planks.
- **Cardio**: 10-15 minutes of brisk walking or jogging.
- **Cool Down**: 10 minutes of static stretching and myofascial release

Incorporate Variety
Variety prevents boredom and challenges different muscle groups. Rotate between these components. It is important to note that if you are inexperienced, you should look to hire a professional personal trainer to ensure proper progression, form, and work out plans to prevent injury and give you external motivation:

1. **Strength Training**: Focus on building muscle with resistance exercises. Include compound movements like deadlifts and bench presses.
2. **Cardio**: Enhance heart health and burn calories with activities like walking, cycling, swimming, or running.
3. **Flexibility and Mobility**: Whatever you do, do NOT skip this because it prevents injury and soreness. Yoga or stretching routines improve range of motion and are beneficial to all aspects of life.

Adjust for Your Goals
- **To Build Muscle**: Prioritize weightlifting with progressive overload, gradually increasing resistance.
- **To Lose Weight**: Combine cardio with high-rep strength exercises to maximize calorie burn. Walking is greatly overlooked and the benefits of using fat for energy is higher at this lower intensity.
- **For Long-Term Health**: Balance strength, cardio, and mobility for overall fitness.

Tips for Staying Committed

Create a Schedule
Block workout times on your calendar as non-negotiable appointments. Aim for consistency, such as exercising three to four days per week. There are many apps that can help you with scheduling your life activities and your workouts. Applications like ToDoist are great for this and can help you collaborate with friends and family to make your health journey contagious to others in your life.

Make Workouts Convenient
Eliminate barriers by choosing accessible routines or locations. Home workouts using bodyweight or minimal equipment can be just as effective as gym sessions. For others, going to the gym helps with motivation because of the feeling of community.

Stay Accountable
Share your goals with friends or join a fitness group for support. Consider hiring a trainer or using a workout app to track progress and stay motivated.

Measure Progress and Adapt
Regularly evaluate your results and adjust routines to avoid plateaus. If you notice strength gains, increase weights or reps. For weight loss, reassess calorie intake and activity levels. Be mindful of your macronutrient intake to ensure you are getting all the nutrients you need.

Long-Term Success

Overcome Obstacles
Life's challenges can derail the best intentions. If you miss a workout, don't dwell on it. Return to your routine as soon as possible.

Celebrate Milestones
Reward yourself for hitting major goals, whether it's new gear, a massage, or a fun outing. Positive reinforcement keeps motivation high.

Keep Evolving
Fitness is a lifelong journey. Experiment with new activities, like hiking or dance classes, to keep things fresh and exciting.

Starting strong and staying consistent with your New Year fitness goals is entirely achievable with a combination of thoughtful planning and determination. Begin by setting clear, actionable goals, crafting effective routines, and surrounding yourself with a supportive environment. For even better results, consider working with a professional trainer who can guide you toward safe and sustainable progress. With the right approach, you can make fitness a lasting part of your lifestyle.

SMART Goals
to a healthy lifestyle

1 SPECIFIC
2 MEASURABLE
3 ACHIEVABLE
4 RELEVANT
5 TIME-BOUND

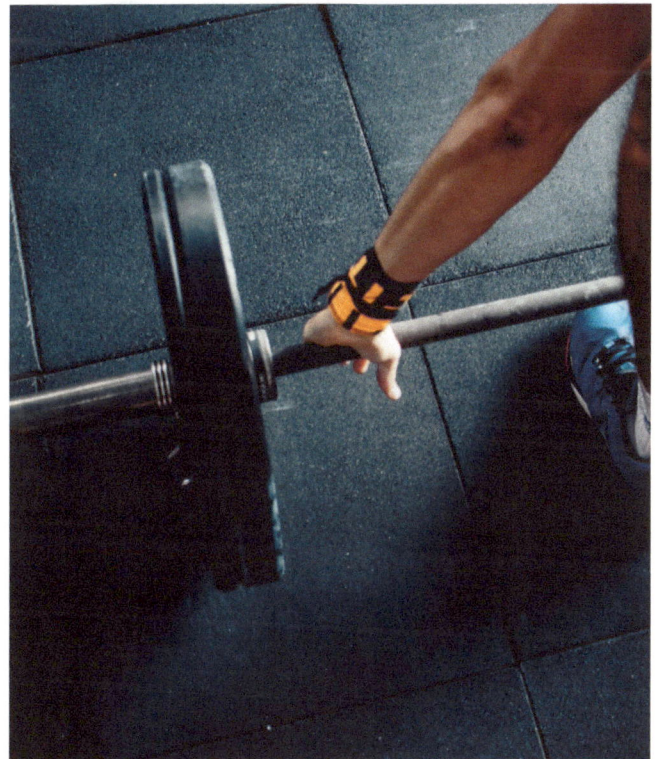

CONNECT WITH JUSTIN
www.aspire2morefitness.com
www.instagram.com/aspire_2more
www.facebook.com/profile.php?id=61568478105095

JOIN OUR COMMUNITY

We believe the future is female and that we are better and stronger together. This group is NOT just for entrepreneurs but for women in general of all ages and from all walks of life.

www.bit.ly/srscommunitygroup

WE ARE
SHE RISES STUDIOS

We are a real-life community of women working to become the best version of themselves to change their lives and make the world a better place.

Group by Hanna J Olivas

She Rises Studios Community

🔒 Private group · 6.4K members

+ Invite   Share   Joined ⌄   ⌄

Discussion   Featured   Members   Events   Media   Files   🔍   ...

Write something...   About

FROM CORPORATE SUCCESS TO SPIRITUAL AWAKENING: VICTORIA STAKELUM'S PATH TO HEALING

by Victoria Stakelum

Victoria Stakelum, a seasoned specialist in emotional healing and the subconscious mind, embarked on her transformative journey when she was drawn back to her innate gifts of insight and healing. From a young age, she sensed a deep connection to intuition, but years of academic and corporate pursuits distanced her from these roots. By 2018, Stakelum began to reconnect with her calling, pursuing a Master's degree in psychology focused on mindfulness and emotion, and delving into alternative healing methods like Reiki and Pranic healing. Despite her success as Deputy Chief Executive in a traditional corporate role, the global pandemic and her evolving spiritual path led her to shift gears fully. Leaving a 20-year career behind, Stakelum embraced her new role in emotional healing and coaching, feeling compelled to support others in their transformative journeys.

Stakelum's approach, now encapsulated in her Chrysalis program, integrates a blend of energy work, emotional healing, and mindset coaching. Her methods address not only the conscious but also the unconscious mind, helping clients dissolve the limiting beliefs and emotional patterns that often impede progress. In her work, she emphasizes the need to release attachments to others' expectations and clear the mind of external influences, empowering clients to identify their own aligned path. From this place of inner clarity and resilience, her clients can pursue genuine goals and take consistent action, even in the face of obstacles.

One powerful success story from Stakelum's Chrysalis program is Yasmine, who, at the start, struggled with severe CPTSD, anxiety, and strained family relationships. Through the program, Yasmine was able to heal, develop a positive self-image, and find personal happiness. Her story embodies the transformative effect of Stakelum's approach, as she not only found love but also cultivated peace within herself, profoundly altering her life's trajectory.

Stakelum's work in uncovering subconscious blocks is further supported by her 'Uncover Your Subconscious Mindset Blocks' quiz, which helps individuals identify personal obstacles across four key *"planes"* she describes: action, emotion, cognition, and spiritual alignment. She believes that success flows when these areas are in harmony.

Her quiz pinpoints where clients might be misaligned and offers strategies to release these blocks, allowing for a more seamless path to success.

Additionally, her work in the field of wellness and entrepreneurship is encapsulated in her writings, which include contributions to anthologies like The Force of Women CEOs, Becoming an Unstoppable Woman Entrepreneur, and Becoming an Unstoppable Woman in Health and Wellness. Each piece draws on her insights into mindset, the critical importance of love and fear in entrepreneurship, and the unconscious stories that often shape our behavior and self-image.

Stakelum's Transformation Ebook offers readers a structured approach to achieving lasting change, beginning with identifying desired life changes, understanding what might be blocking progress, and then focusing on building a mindset aligned with personal goals. Through a combination of reflective journaling, vision setting, and actionable strategies, her ebook aims to equip readers with practical tools for long-term transformation across various aspects of their lives, including health, career, and relationships.

In essence, Victoria Stakelum's work is a holistic fusion of psychological insight, energy healing, and actionable strategies. Her dedication to helping clients uncover and reshape the subconscious narratives that hold them back has empowered countless individuals to embrace change, heal, and achieve authentic success.

CONNECT WITH VICTORIA

www.thesuccesssmith.com
https://getsuccess.scoreapp.com
https://www.connect.thesuccesssmith.com/transform

A FRESH START: BREAKING MENTAL BARRIERS AND EMBRACING CHANGE

By Danielle Thompson, Ph.D.

The start of a new year often carries a mix of hope and hesitation. While the promise of a fresh start is invigorating, the mental barriers that hold us back can feel overwhelming. Fear of failure, self-doubt, and deeply ingrained limiting beliefs can prevent us from stepping into the lives we envision for ourselves. Yet, the stories of those who've navigated these challenges show that breaking through isn't about eliminating fear but transforming how we respond to it.

Through my work with the Seismic Imprint project, I've encountered remarkable individuals who have turned adversity into opportunity, building resilience and embracing change. Their journeys reveal a universal truth: the process of overcoming mental barriers is personal, but it begins with awareness, intention, and action.

Name the Barrier

The first step in breaking mental barriers is acknowledging them. Often, we allow these obstacles to operate silently, influencing our decisions and limiting our potential. By naming them—whether it's fear of failure, perfectionism, or imposter syndrome—we take the first step toward disempowering them.

One participant in the Seismic Imprint project shared, *"When I finally admitted what I was afraid of, it stopped being this invisible weight I couldn't explain. It became something I could address."* Naming your barrier gives it a shape you can confront rather than an amorphous force that controls you.

Try this:
Take a quiet moment to reflect on what's holding you back. Write it down. Naming your barrier is the first step to releasing its grip.

Reframe Your Perspective

A shift in perspective can be transformative. Instead of viewing challenges as threats, consider them opportunities for growth.

If failure looms large, reframe it as a learning experience rather than a verdict on your abilities. Instead of focusing on what could go wrong, ask, *"What could I gain from trying?"*

This shift isn't about ignoring difficulties but about seeing them through a lens of possibility rather than limitation. Those in the Seismic Imprint project repeatedly emphasized how small mindset adjustments opened doors they once thought permanently closed.

Try this:
The next time a negative thought arises, pause and challenge it. Replace it with a question or statement rooted in growth and possibility.

Lean Into Your Support System

No one needs to face these challenges alone, and often, the encouragement of others provides the strength to take the first step. Whether it's a mentor, a trusted friend, or a community of like-minded individuals, having people who believe in your potential can make all the difference.

As one participant reflected, *"In moments of doubt, I leaned on those who reminded me of my worth. Their belief in me helped me believe in myself."*

Try this:
Identify one person you trust who can support your journey. Share your goals with them and ask for their encouragement and feedback as you work to overcome your mental barriers.

Take One Bold Step

Progress often starts with one small, bold step. It might be applying for a new role, enrolling in a course, or speaking up when you'd normally stay silent. The act itself matters less than the courage it represents. Boldness creates momentum, and that momentum is a catalyst for change.

One lesson from the Seismic Imprint project is clear: action, no matter how small, signals to yourself and the world that you're ready to grow.

Try this:
What's one small but bold step you can take this week? Write it down and commit to it.

Celebrate the Journey

Transformation is a journey, not a destination. Each step forward, each challenge faced, and each barrier overcome deserves acknowledgment. This practice builds confidence and reinforces the belief that growth is possible.

In the words of another Seismic Imprint participant, *"Recognizing my small wins kept me going when the big picture felt overwhelming. Each step added up to a bigger change than I ever imagined."*

Try this:
At the end of each day, write down one thing you're proud of. Over time, these small moments of pride will build a foundation of confidence and self-belief.

A Vital Year Ahead
Breaking mental barriers and embracing change is deeply personal, but it's also universal in its potential. As we step into this new year, we have the opportunity to redefine what's possible—not by eliminating fear and doubt but by meeting them with clarity, persistence, and action.

The individuals of Seismic Imprint have shown that resilience isn't about being fearless; it's about choosing to move forward despite the fear. This year, commit to embracing the fresh start in front of you. Name your barriers, reframe your perspective, lean on your support system, take bold steps, and celebrate your progress.

A fresh start isn't a magical reset. It's a choice. It's the decision to believe that change is possible and the willingness to take the steps to make it happen. As we enter 2025, let's step into the year with vitality, confidence, and the knowledge that our best days are ahead of us.

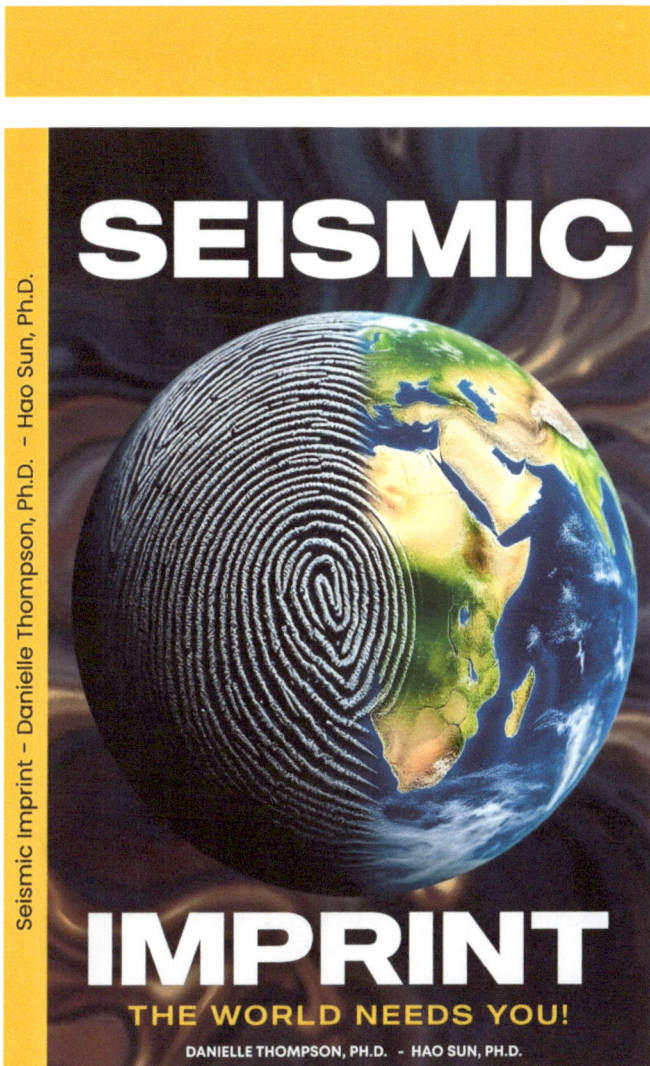

Seismic Imprint – Danielle Thompson, Ph.D. – Hao Sun, Ph.D.

SEISMIC

IMPRINT
THE WORLD NEEDS YOU!
DANIELLE THOMPSON, PH.D. - HAO SUN, PH.D.

CONNECT WITH DANIELLE

www.seismicImprint.com
www.instagram.com/seismicimprint
www.facebook.com/profile.php?id=61564060739412
www.tiktok.com/@seismic.imprint
www.linkedin.com/posts/seismic-imprint

The SHE RISES STUDIOS
PODCAST

The She Rises Studios podcast is dedicated to empowering women like you to reach their full potential and live their best lives. With inspiring stories, insightful interviews, and practical advice from experts in different industries, our podcast is your go-to source for information, inspiration, and motivation. Join us as we explore topics like:

- Overcoming self-doubt and limiting beliefs
- Building and running a successful business
- Building confidence and Self-esteem
- Navigating career transitions
- Starting and growing a business
- Balancing work and family life
- Improving physical and mental health
- Finding meaning and purpose in life
- So many more

Our guests include successful entrepreneurs, inspiring thought leaders, and everyday women who have overcome challenges and achieved their dreams. Each episode is packed with actionable tips and strategies to help you take your life to the next level.

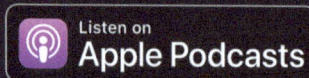

Listen on Apple Podcasts

Listen on Spotify

I'M JEN RIGLEY, FOUNDER OF FLOURISHING OVER FIFTY

It's January! The hustle and bustle of the holidays is over and we are settling back into our routines. In many areas of the country it is cold and wet, and everywhere the sun is low on the horizon - it's dark when we wake up and when we leave the office. It's also the time when many of us hibernate and are alone with our thoughts. We can start to feel down as we spend less time with others, less time in the sun and less time being active.

But the opposite is also true -- we have more time to dive deep into our desires and focus on activities that are most meaningful to us. A little more me time and a little less time spent on everyone else. A journal, a fire, a bath, a lit candle - how scrumptious is that? I invite you to step into what feels most good to you during these winter days - take the time to pamper, to heal, to cultivate joy in your special way.

There was a time in my life when I was caught up in my own personal vortex - a swirling mass of challenges and change. I was downsized out of my executive position, my mother fell ill, and I faced a breast cancer diagnosis. But as I navigated these hardships, I realized something powerful: even after significant trauma, we can choose to flourish.

That's when the idea of Flourishing Over Fifty, and The Flourish JourneyTM was forged - a vision for inspiration and resources, where women in midlife can come together, lift each other up, hold space and share our stories. When I was facing my hardest moments, I longed for a community like this, a place that felt like home even online.

The Flourish JourneyTM, my framework for overcoming challenges and trauma so you can create a new story for your life has 7 steps, but the first is the most important one - and it fits so well with our winter lives.

Understanding that starting on the path to create a new story for your life is not as easy as *"just change your mindset"*, this process takes you on a journey as you walk through the steps of designing your new story.

This first step in The Flourish Journey ™ is all about creating the foundation. I recommend committing to spending 3 minutes on the following activities to set the foundation for your day:

- **Sit in Stillness** - spend 1 minute quieting your mind and taking some deep breaths. This is when you put your phone in silent mode and turn off the TV.
- **Set your Intention** - spend 1 minute setting your intention for the day. This is not about accomplishing your to-do list, it is more about how you want to feel, or how you want to make others feel.
- **Hold Gratitude** - spend 1 minute thinking, feeling, writing, drawing or painting what you are grateful for.

By committing to these 3 activities each day (just 3 minutes a day), you have the opportunity to change the trajectory not only of your day, but you have the opportunity to change the trajectory of your life.

Flourishing Over FiftyTM is more than an idea, it's a reminder that in midlife, we're just beginning to tap into our true strength. We're here to support, inspire, and help each other through. Here's to our resilience, our joy, and to flourishing over fifty.

Sign-up at *www.flourishingoverfifty.com* to receive our newsletter so you, too, can start creating a new story for your life.

CONNECT WITH JEN

www.instagram.com/flourishingoverfifty
www.facebook.com/flourishingoverfifty
www.flourishingoverfifty.com/subscribe-page

Tired of Guessing?

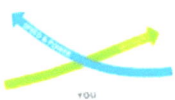

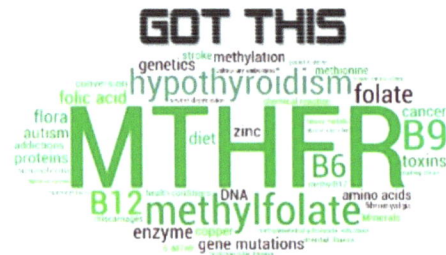

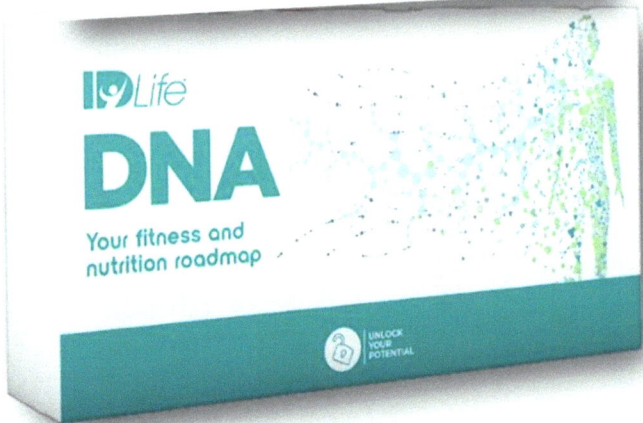

When it comes to YOUR Fitness and Nutrition, we unlock the secrets of your DNA with our comprehensive DNA Kit from Jules Body Shoppe. This isn't your typical paternity or family line DNA test – it's a personalized roadmap to optimizing your health and well-being.

https://julesbodyshoppe.idlife.com

THRIVE TRANSFORM

ELEVATE YOUR LIFE !

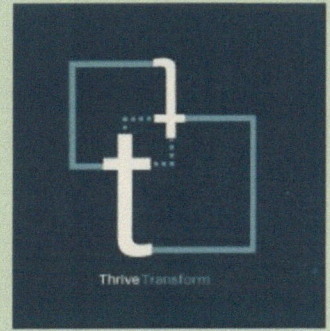

Thrive Transform

Life Coach
Your Life, Your Blueprint!

PATHFINDING
Navigate Career Moves and Personal transitions

DECODING THE SIGNS
Understand Fatigue, Anxiety & Relationship Dynamics

BEYOND THE 9-5
Unleash your Potential, Create a Meaningful & Purposeful Life

TRANSFORMATION
Mater tools for Professional & Personal Growth

EMPOWER YOUR JOURNEY

First 10 "She Rises,"members receive 10% of Packages. Book FREE 45 min call TODAY!

WHY ME?

As a single parent, a professional, & someone who's walked through transitions & challenges, I bring not just expertise but real-life experience to the table. Customized Package; using Somatic techniques; MINDFULNESS, BREATHING, VISUALIZATION; I will help you gain Clarity, Find Purpose & bring Changes in your LIFE!

Stop Surviving, & Start Thriving!!!

transformthrive853@gmail.com

FROM DIVORCE TO EMPOWERMENT: EMBRACE YOUR NEW BEGINNING WITH SOURAYA CHRISTINE

Souraya Christine's journey through five marriages and divorces is not just a story of loss—it's a story of transformation, resilience, and purpose. Instead of allowing her struggles to define her, she channeled her experiences into a powerful platform dedicated to helping women recover from relationship trauma and rediscover their inner strength. Her mission is clear: to empower women to reclaim their emotional power and step into the happiness they truly deserve.

Souraya's personal story serves as the foundation of her work. She learned through her own healing journey that much of her pain came from giving away her power to external circumstances and the actions of others. Each divorce became a chapter of growth, teaching her crucial lessons about resilience, self-worth, and the power of choosing joy. She found purpose in transforming her challenges into opportunities to help other women see that their past does not have to shape their future. *"Happiness truly is a choice,"* Souraya often says, a message born from her own experiences and the desire to show others that healing is possible.

As an ordained pastor and the founder of the L.I.L.A.C. Women's Ministry, Souraya brings a holistic approach to recovery. She combines spiritual wisdom with practical psychological strategies, creating a safe space for emotional and spiritual healing. Her coaching draws on Philippians 4:6-8, a verse that encourages focusing on what is pure, lovely, and praiseworthy, merging biblical guidance with practical, science-backed psychological insights. This blend of faith-based wisdom and actionable advice helps women heal on multiple levels—emotional, spiritual, and mental.

In her bestselling book Damaged Goods: A Woman's Guide to Surviving Divorce… and Other Matters, Souraya delivers a crucial message: women are not *"damaged goods"* but individuals in progress. She challenges women to reclaim their stories, reinforcing that while we can't control life's circumstances, we can control our responses. A key takeaway from the book is embracing contentment in the present moment while striving for positive change. *"Healing is a choice we make daily,"* she encourages, empowering women to take control of their journey, one step at a time.

Souraya's commitment extends beyond personal coaching and writing. In September 2023, she launched the W.O.M.E.N. in Leadership Conference Tour, a groundbreaking initiative aimed at addressing mental health, self-care, and emotional resilience in leadership. Through this tour, she connected with professional women across nine states, encouraging them to prioritize self-care as the foundation for their personal and professional success. *"You can't pour from an empty cup,"* she reminds her audience. By fostering emotionally healthy leaders, Souraya creates a ripple effect that positively impacts entire organizations and communities.

For women feeling trapped in the aftermath of divorce, Souraya offers a powerful message of hope. She acknowledges their struggles but assures them that a brighter future is possible. *"Start small,"* she advises. *"Focus on one moment at a time where you can choose joy."* Surround yourself with supportive communities, seek guidance through coaching or ministry, and remember that healing isn't about erasing the past—it's about releasing its power over your future.

If you're ready to transform your divorce experience into a journey of empowerment, resilience, and self-discovery, Souraya Christine's Divorce Recovery Coaching for Women is here to guide you. With a compassionate and practical approach, personalized coaching sessions, and a commitment to seeing women thrive, Souraya offers the support and tools you need to reclaim your life and joy.

Available for in-person sessions in Las Vegas, virtual coaching worldwide, and travel sessions upon request, Souraya is dedicated to empowering women at every stage of their recovery journey.

Start your transformation today and embrace a vibrant new chapter of your life. Visit www.sourayachristine.com to learn more about Divorce Recovery Coaching for Women and take the first step toward a future where you don't just survive—you thrive.

"Your divorce is a chapter in your story, not the end of it."
– Souraya Christine

CONNECT WITH SOURAYA

www.linkedin.com/in/sourayaspeaks
www.facebook.com/souraya.christine
www.instagram.com/sourayaspeaks
www.sourayachristine.com

FENIX TV
WATCH THE
EMMYS PREMIER EVENT
LIVE ON FENIX TV
FROM BEHIND-THE-SCENES PREP TO OUR EMMYS WEEK GIFTING SUITE AND THE 76TH ANNUAL PRIMETIME EMMYS!
www.fenixtv.app

www.ingramcontent.com/pod-product-compliance
Lightning Source LLC
Chambersburg PA
CBHW061142030426
42335CB00002B/74

9781960136541